Copyright © 2016 by Dominique Broadway.

All rights reserved.

No part of this publication may be reproduced, stored, or transmitted in any form or by any means, electronic, mechanical, photocopying, recording, scanning, or otherwise, except as permited under Section 107 or 108 of the 1976 United States Copyright Act, without the prior written permission of the author. Requests to the author and publisher for permission should be addressed to the following email: info@dominiquebroadway.com.

Limitation of liability/disclaimer of warranty: While the publisher and author have used their best efforts in preparing this guide and workbook, they make no representations or warranties with respect to the accuracy or completeness of the contents of this document and specifically disclaim any implied warranties of merchantability or fitness for particular purpose. No warranty may be created or extended by sales representatives, promoters, or written sales materials.

The advice and strategies contained herein may not be suitable for your situation. You should consult with a professional where appropriate. Neither the publisher nor author shall be liable for any loss of profit or any other commercial damages, including but not limited to special, incidental, consequential, or other damages.

One of the many lessons I have learned in my years as an entrepreneur and long before, is the importance of really making it happen. Yes, talking about what you want to do is great and all, but having a action plan to make some things happen is how you quickly and efficiently begin to reach your goals and bring your *Dreams2Reality*!

The Brain Dump sheets will help you get all of your ideas out of your brain onto paper! The Action Plans can be used for daily, weekly, monthly or annual goals. The Monthly Bill Checklist will not only help you further organize your bills, but will also provide you with a visual view of your bills and the dates they are due to avoid late and overdraft fees. The Savings Plan & Tracker is the perfect tool to keep track of your saving progress.

Enjoy this workbook that will help you tackle your personal, business and financial goals.
Now, Let's Make It Happen!

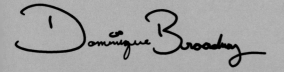

YOUR *official* GOAL SETTING
GUIDE

BRAIN DUMP:
Take 15-20 minutes, turn of all distractions and write down any ideas, goals or anything that you want to make happen.

MAKE IT HAPPEN ACTION PLAN
1. Write down a goal or idea from your Brain Dump in the goal section.
2. Write the cost or price to reach this goal (if necessary).
3. Write the actions that you need to take to turn this Dream2Reality.
4. Write the date that each action item needs to be completed, beside the respective action.

ACCOUNTABILITY:
- Set a reminder in your phone or calendar to ensure you accomplish your actions.
- Tell a friend about the goals you want to accomplish, so they will help to hold you accountable.

brain dump

DATE:

THE
make it happen
ACTION PLAN

GOAL:

ACTION ITEM	GOAL DATE
☐	
☐	
☐	
☐	

GOAL:

ACTION ITEM	GOAL DATE
☐	
☐	
☐	
☐	

GOAL:

ACTION ITEM	GOAL DATE
☐	
☐	
☐	
☐	

brain dump

DATE:

If you can dream it, you can achieve it. — Zig Ziglar

THE
make it happen
ACTION PLAN

GOAL:

ACTION ITEM	GOAL DATE
☐	
☐	
☐	
☐	

GOAL:

ACTION ITEM	GOAL DATE
☐	
☐	
☐	
☐	

GOAL:

ACTION ITEM	GOAL DATE
☐	
☐	
☐	
☐	

brain dump

DATE:

THE *make it happen* ACTION PLAN

GOAL:

ACTION ITEM	GOAL DATE
☐	
☐	
☐	
☐	

GOAL:

ACTION ITEM	GOAL DATE
☐	
☐	
☐	
☐	

GOAL:

ACTION ITEM	GOAL DATE
☐	
☐	
☐	
☐	

brain dump

DATE:

THE
make it happen
ACTION PLAN

GOAL:

ACTION ITEM	GOAL DATE
☐	
☐	
☐	
☐	

GOAL:

ACTION ITEM	GOAL DATE
☐	
☐	
☐	
☐	

GOAL:

ACTION ITEM	GOAL DATE
☐	
☐	
☐	
☐	

brain dump

DATE:

Whether you think you can or you think you can't, you're right. — Henry Ford

THE *make it happen*
ACTION PLAN

GOAL:

ACTION ITEM	GOAL DATE
☐	
☐	
☐	
☐	

GOAL:

ACTION ITEM	GOAL DATE
☐	
☐	
☐	
☐	

GOAL:

ACTION ITEM	GOAL DATE
☐	
☐	
☐	
☐	

brain dump

DATE:

Great minds discuss ideas; average minds discuss events; small minds discuss people.- Eleanor Roosevelt

THE
make it happen
ACTION PLAN

GOAL:

ACTION ITEM	GOAL DATE
☐	
☐	
☐	
☐	

GOAL:

ACTION ITEM	GOAL DATE
☐	
☐	
☐	
☐	

GOAL:

ACTION ITEM	GOAL DATE
☐	
☐	
☐	
☐	

brain dump

DATE:

THE *make it happen* ACTION PLAN

GOAL:

ACTION ITEM	GOAL DATE
☐	
☐	
☐	
☐	

GOAL:

ACTION ITEM	GOAL DATE
☐	
☐	
☐	
☐	

GOAL:

ACTION ITEM	GOAL DATE
☐	
☐	
☐	
☐	

brain dump

DATE:

THE *make it happen* ACTION PLAN

GOAL:

ACTION ITEM	GOAL DATE
☐	
☐	
☐	
☐	

GOAL:

ACTION ITEM	GOAL DATE
☐	
☐	
☐	
☐	

GOAL:

ACTION ITEM	GOAL DATE
☐	
☐	
☐	
☐	

brain dump

DATE:

THE
make it happen
ACTION PLAN

GOAL:

ACTION ITEM	GOAL DATE
☐	
☐	
☐	
☐	

GOAL:

ACTION ITEM	GOAL DATE
☐	
☐	
☐	
☐	

GOAL:

ACTION ITEM	GOAL DATE
☐	
☐	
☐	
☐	

brain dump

DATE:

Focus all your life energy to whatever goal you set yourself to achieve. - Banyambiki Habyarimana

THE
make it happen
ACTION PLAN

GOAL:

ACTION ITEM	GOAL DATE
☐	
☐	
☐	
☐	

GOAL:

ACTION ITEM	GOAL DATE
☐	
☐	
☐	
☐	

GOAL:

ACTION ITEM	GOAL DATE
☐	
☐	
☐	
☐	

brain dump

DATE:

THE
make it happen
ACTION PLAN

GOAL:

ACTION ITEM   GOAL DATE

☐

☐

☐

☐

GOAL:

ACTION ITEM   GOAL DATE

☐

☐

☐

☐

GOAL:

ACTION ITEM   GOAL DATE

☐

☐

☐

☐

brain dump

DATE:

Dreams are extremely important. You can't do it unless you imagine it. —George Lucas

THE make it happen
ACTION PLAN

GOAL:

ACTION ITEM	GOAL DATE
☐	
☐	
☐	
☐	

GOAL:

ACTION ITEM	GOAL DATE
☐	
☐	
☐	
☐	

GOAL:

ACTION ITEM	GOAL DATE
☐	
☐	
☐	
☐	

brain dump

DATE:

A mediocre idea that generates enthusiasm will go further then a great idea that inspires no one. -Mary Kay Ash

THE *make it happen* ACTION PLAN

GOAL:

ACTION ITEM	GOAL DATE
☐	
☐	
☐	
☐	

GOAL:

ACTION ITEM	GOAL DATE
☐	
☐	
☐	
☐	

GOAL:

ACTION ITEM	GOAL DATE
☐	
☐	
☐	
☐	

brain dump

DATE:

I don't dream at night, I dream all day; I dream for a living. -Steven Spielberg

THE *make it happen*
ACTION PLAN

GOAL:

ACTION ITEM	GOAL DATE
☐	
☐	
☐	
☐	

GOAL:

ACTION ITEM	GOAL DATE
☐	
☐	
☐	
☐	

GOAL:

ACTION ITEM	GOAL DATE
☐	
☐	
☐	
☐	

brain dump

DATE:

THE *make it happen*
ACTION PLAN

GOAL:

ACTION ITEM	GOAL DATE
☐	
☐	
☐	
☐	

GOAL:

ACTION ITEM	GOAL DATE
☐	
☐	
☐	
☐	

GOAL:

ACTION ITEM	GOAL DATE
☐	
☐	
☐	
☐	

brain dump

DATE:

You can do anything as long as you have the passion, the drive, the focus, and the support. — Sabrina Bryan

THE *make it happen* ACTION PLAN

GOAL:

ACTION ITEM	GOAL DATE
☐	
☐	
☐	
☐	

GOAL:

ACTION ITEM	GOAL DATE
☐	
☐	
☐	
☐	

GOAL:

ACTION ITEM	GOAL DATE
☐	
☐	
☐	
☐	

brain dump

DATE:

All our dreams can come true if we have the courage to pursue them. -Walt Disney

THE
make it happen
ACTION PLAN

GOAL:

ACTION ITEM	GOAL DATE
☐	
☐	
☐	
☐	

GOAL:

ACTION ITEM	GOAL DATE
☐	
☐	
☐	
☐	

GOAL:

ACTION ITEM	GOAL DATE
☐	
☐	
☐	
☐	

brain dump

DATE:

THE *make it happen* ACTION PLAN

GOAL:

ACTION ITEM	GOAL DATE
☐	
☐	
☐	
☐	

GOAL:

ACTION ITEM	GOAL DATE
☐	
☐	
☐	
☐	

GOAL:

ACTION ITEM	GOAL DATE
☐	
☐	
☐	
☐	

brain dump

DATE:

THE make it happen
ACTION PLAN

GOAL:

ACTION ITEM	GOAL DATE
☐	
☐	
☐	
☐	

GOAL:

ACTION ITEM	GOAL DATE
☐	
☐	
☐	
☐	

GOAL:

ACTION ITEM	GOAL DATE
☐	
☐	
☐	
☐	

brain dump

DATE:

try not to become a person of success, but rather try
to become a person of value. - Albert Einstein

THE
make it happen
ACTION PLAN

GOAL:

ACTION ITEM   GOAL DATE

☐

☐

☐

☐

GOAL:

ACTION ITEM   GOAL DATE

☐

☐

☐

☐

GOAL:

ACTION ITEM   GOAL DATE

☐

☐

☐

☐

brain dump

DATE:

It is precisely the possibility of realizing a dream
that makes life interesting. -Paulo Coelho

THE
make it happen
ACTION PLAN

GOAL:

ACTION ITEM	GOAL DATE
☐	
☐	
☐	
☐	

GOAL:

ACTION ITEM	GOAL DATE
☐	
☐	
☐	
☐	

GOAL:

ACTION ITEM	GOAL DATE
☐	
☐	
☐	
☐	

brain dump

DATE:

the future you see is the future you get. — Robert G. Allen

THE
make it happen
ACTION PLAN

GOAL:

ACTION ITEM	GOAL DATE
☐	
☐	
☐	
☐	

GOAL:

ACTION ITEM	GOAL DATE
☐	
☐	
☐	
☐	

GOAL:

ACTION ITEM	GOAL DATE
☐	
☐	
☐	
☐	

brain dump

DATE:

to accomplish great things, we must not only act, but also dream;
not only plan, but also believe. - Anatole France

THE *make it happen*
ACTION PLAN

GOAL:

	ACTION ITEM	GOAL DATE
☐		
☐		
☐		
☐		

GOAL:

	ACTION ITEM	GOAL DATE
☐		
☐		
☐		
☐		

GOAL:

	ACTION ITEM	GOAL DATE
☐		
☐		
☐		
☐		

brain dump

DATE:

THE *make it happen*
ACTION PLAN

GOAL:

ACTION ITEM	GOAL DATE
☐	
☐	
☐	
☐	

GOAL:

ACTION ITEM	GOAL DATE
☐	
☐	
☐	
☐	

GOAL:

ACTION ITEM	GOAL DATE
☐	
☐	
☐	
☐	

brain dump

DATE:

THE
make it happen
ACTION PLAN

GOAL:

ACTION ITEM	GOAL DATE
☐	
☐	
☐	
☐	

GOAL:

ACTION ITEM	GOAL DATE
☐	
☐	
☐	
☐	

GOAL:

ACTION ITEM	GOAL DATE
☐	
☐	
☐	
☐	

brain dump

DATE:

THE *make it happen* ACTION PLAN

GOAL:

ACTION ITEM	GOAL DATE
☐	
☐	
☐	
☐	

GOAL:

ACTION ITEM	GOAL DATE
☐	
☐	
☐	
☐	

GOAL:

ACTION ITEM	GOAL DATE
☐	
☐	
☐	
☐	

brain dump

DATE:

Logic will get you from A to B. Imagination will take you everywhere. - Albert Einstein

THE
make it happen
ACTION PLAN

GOAL:

ACTION ITEM	GOAL DATE
☐	
☐	
☐	
☐	

GOAL:

ACTION ITEM	GOAL DATE
☐	
☐	
☐	
☐	

GOAL:

ACTION ITEM	GOAL DATE
☐	
☐	
☐	
☐	

brain dump

DATE:

THE
make it happen
ACTION PLAN

GOAL:

ACTION ITEM	GOAL DATE
☐	
☐	
☐	
☐	

GOAL:

ACTION ITEM	GOAL DATE
☐	
☐	
☐	
☐	

GOAL:

ACTION ITEM	GOAL DATE
☐	
☐	
☐	
☐	

brain dump

DATE:

No matter what people tell you, words and ideas can change the world. – Robin Williams

THE *make it happen*
ACTION PLAN

GOAL:

ACTION ITEM   GOAL DATE

☐

☐

☐

☐

GOAL:

ACTION ITEM   GOAL DATE

☐

☐

☐

☐

GOAL:

ACTION ITEM   GOAL DATE

☐

☐

☐

☐

brain dump

DATE:

the difficulty lies not so much in developing new ideas as in escaping from old ones. - John Maynard Keynes

THE
make it happen
ACTION PLAN

GOAL:

ACTION ITEM   GOAL DATE

☐

☐

☐

☐

GOAL:

ACTION ITEM   GOAL DATE

☐

☐

☐

☐

GOAL:

ACTION ITEM   GOAL DATE

☐

☐

☐

☐

brain dump

DATE:

THE
make it happen
ACTION PLAN

GOAL:

ACTION ITEM	GOAL DATE
☐	
☐	
☐	
☐	

GOAL:

ACTION ITEM	GOAL DATE
☐	
☐	
☐	
☐	

GOAL:

ACTION ITEM	GOAL DATE
☐	
☐	
☐	
☐	

brain dump

DATE:

Money never starts an idea; it is the idea that starts the money. - William J. Cameron

THE *make it happen* ACTION PLAN

GOAL:

ACTION ITEM   GOAL DATE

☐

☐

☐

☐

GOAL:

ACTION ITEM   GOAL DATE

☐

☐

☐

☐

GOAL:

ACTION ITEM   GOAL DATE

☐

☐

☐

☐

brain dump

DATE:

THE *make it happen* ACTION PLAN

GOAL:

ACTION ITEM   GOAL DATE

☐

☐

☐

☐

GOAL:

ACTION ITEM   GOAL DATE

☐

☐

☐

☐

GOAL:

ACTION ITEM   GOAL DATE

☐

☐

☐

☐

brain dump

DATE:

I am not a product of my circumstances. I am a product of my decisions. - Stephen Covey

THE
make it happen
ACTION PLAN

GOAL:

ACTION ITEM   GOAL DATE

☐

☐

☐

☐

GOAL:

ACTION ITEM   GOAL DATE

☐

☐

☐

☐

GOAL:

ACTION ITEM   GOAL DATE

☐

☐

☐

☐

brain dump

DATE:

the question isn't who is going to let me; it's who is going to stop me. —Ayn Rand

THE *make it happen*
ACTION PLAN

GOAL:

ACTION ITEM	GOAL DATE
☐	
☐	
☐	
☐	

GOAL:

ACTION ITEM	GOAL DATE
☐	
☐	
☐	
☐	

GOAL:

ACTION ITEM	GOAL DATE
☐	
☐	
☐	
☐	

THE *financial* CONVERSATION

The topic of money is still very taboo! No one talks about how much money they make, their credit scores, who they bank with and overall avoid this topic all together. That has to stop! You can use the My Financial Inventory worksheet to begin documenting your current financial situation and the Family Financial Inventory worksheets for your loved loves. This should not only allow you to have an overall understanding of your finances, but also help you provoke the conversations with your loved ones. So in the event that something happens to them or yourself, you are not scrambling to find their bank accounts, retirement accounts or life insurance policies.

NOW, LET'S HAVE A FINANCIAL CONVERSATION!

#MONEYTALK

MY
finances

MY financial INVENTORY

Use this worksheet to keep track of the current status of your financial life. You should use a pencil as things may change, or keep this information in a digital document. Share with your loved ones.

HAVE BANK ACCOUNTS WITH:

NAME OF BANK	ACCOUNT #	ACCOUNT TYPE

HAVE INVESTMENT ACCOUNTS WITH:

INVESTMENT COMPANY	ACCOUNT #	ACCOUNT TYPE

HAVE RETIREMENT ACCOUNTS WITH:

RETIREMENT ACCOUNT NAME	ACCOUNT #	ACCOUNT TYPE

MY *financial* INVENTORY

I HAVE LIFE INSURANCE WITH:

INSURANCE COMPANY	POLICY #	DEATH BENEFIT

I HAVE OTHER INSURANCES WITH:

INSURANCE COMPANY	POLICY #	DEATH BENEFIT

I HAVE PERSONAL PROPERTY:

PROPERTY DESCRIPTION	VALUE	OTHER INFO

financial INVENTORY

Use this worksheet to keep track of the current status of your financial life. You should use a pencil as things may change, or keep this information in a digital document. Share with your loved ones.

I HAVE BANK ACCOUNTS WITH:

NAME OF BANK	ACCOUNT #	ACCOUNT TYPE

I HAVE INVESTMENT ACCOUNTS WITH:

INVESTMENT COMPANY	ACCOUNT #	ACCOUNT TYPE

I HAVE RETIREMENT ACCOUNTS WITH:

RETIREMENT ACCOUNT NAME	ACCOUNT #	ACCOUNT TYPE

MY *financial* INVENTORY

I HAVE LIFE INSURANCE WITH:

INSURANCE COMPANY	POLICY #	DEATH BENEFIT

I HAVE OTHER INSURANCES WITH:

INSURANCE COMPANY	POLICY #	DEATH BENEFIT

I HAVE PERSONAL PROPERTY:

PROPERTY DESCRIPTION	VALUE	OTHER INFO

budget

_____ 's budget

1. YOUR INCOME

TAKE HOME PAY (WAGES AND TIPS)	
ADDITIONAL INCOME (RENTAL INCOME, PART-TIME JOB, ETC.)	
TOTAL INCOME	$

2. YOUR EXPENSES

HOUSING (RENT & MORTAGE)	
UTILITIES (GAS, ELECTRIC, HEAT, WATER, ETC.)	
CABLE/TV/INTERNET	
HOME PHONE/CELLPHONE	
GROCERIES	
EATING OUT	
PUBLIC TRANSPORTATION	
AUTO (GAS, REPAIRS, PARKING, INSURANCE, ETC.)	
ENTERTAINMENT/ VACATION	
OTHER DISCRETIONARY (HOBBIES, PERSONAL CARE, ETC.)	
SHOPPING & CLOTHING	
GIFTS/DONATIONS	
STUDENT LOANS	
AUTO LOANS	
CREDIT CARD PAYMENTS	
SAVINGS	
TOTAL EXPENSES	$

3. BOTTOMLINE

INCOME MINUS EXPENSES	$

budget

_____ 's budget

1. YOUR INCOME	
TAKE HOME PAY (WAGES AND TIPS)	
ADDITIONAL INCOME (RENTAL INCOME, PART-TIME JOB, ETC.)	
TOTAL INCOME	$

2. YOUR EXPENSES	
HOUSING (RENT & MORTAGE)	
UTILITIES (GAS, ELECTRIC, HEAT, WATER, ETC.)	
CABLE/TV/INTERNET	
HOME PHONE/CELLPHONE	
GROCERIES	
EATING OUT	
PUBLIC TRANSPORTATION	
AUTO (GAS, REPAIRS, PARKING, INSURANCE, ETC.)	
ENTERTAINMENT/ VACATION	
OTHER DISCRETIONARY (HOBBIES, PERSONAL CARE, ETC.)	
SHOPPING & CLOTHING	
GIFTS/DONATIONS	
STUDENT LOANS	
AUTO LOANS	
CREDIT CARD PAYMENTS	
SAVINGS	
TOTAL EXPENSES	$

3. BOTTOMLINE	
INCOME MINUS EXPENSES	$

monthly
BILL CHECKLIST

BILL	DUE DATE	AMOUNT	JAN	FEB	MAR	APR	JUN	JULY	AUG	SEPT	OCT	NOV	DEC
			☐	☐	☐	☐	☐	☐	☐	☐	☐	☐	☐
			☐	☐	☐	☐	☐	☐	☐	☐	☐	☐	☐
			☐	☐	☐	☐	☐	☐	☐	☐	☐	☐	☐
			☐	☐	☐	☐	☐	☐	☐	☐	☐	☐	☐
			☐	☐	☐	☐	☐	☐	☐	☐	☐	☐	☐
			☐	☐	☐	☐	☐	☐	☐	☐	☐	☐	☐
			☐	☐	☐	☐	☐	☐	☐	☐	☐	☐	☐
			☐	☐	☐	☐	☐	☐	☐	☐	☐	☐	☐
			☐	☐	☐	☐	☐	☐	☐	☐	☐	☐	☐
			☐	☐	☐	☐	☐	☐	☐	☐	☐	☐	☐
			☐	☐	☐	☐	☐	☐	☐	☐	☐	☐	☐
			☐	☐	☐	☐	☐	☐	☐	☐	☐	☐	☐
			☐	☐	☐	☐	☐	☐	☐	☐	☐	☐	☐
			☐	☐	☐	☐	☐	☐	☐	☐	☐	☐	☐
			☐	☐	☐	☐	☐	☐	☐	☐	☐	☐	☐
			☐	☐	☐	☐	☐	☐	☐	☐	☐	☐	☐
			☐	☐	☐	☐	☐	☐	☐	☐	☐	☐	☐
			☐	☐	☐	☐	☐	☐	☐	☐	☐	☐	☐
			☐	☐	☐	☐	☐	☐	☐	☐	☐	☐	☐
			☐	☐	☐	☐	☐	☐	☐	☐	☐	☐	☐
			☐	☐	☐	☐	☐	☐	☐	☐	☐	☐	☐
			☐	☐	☐	☐	☐	☐	☐	☐	☐	☐	☐
			☐	☐	☐	☐	☐	☐	☐	☐	☐	☐	☐
			☐	☐	☐	☐	☐	☐	☐	☐	☐	☐	☐
			☐	☐	☐	☐	☐	☐	☐	☐	☐	☐	☐
			☐	☐	☐	☐	☐	☐	☐	☐	☐	☐	☐
			☐	☐	☐	☐	☐	☐	☐	☐	☐	☐	☐

HOW TO USE YOUR
savings plan
TRACKER

SAVINGS PLAN & TRACKER

1. Write your current account balance in the respective savings balance column based on the month you are starting.

2. Add any categories that add extra money to your savings or reduce your savings balance. This can be things such as a tax refund or a bonus from work that will increase your savings or a vacation that would take money out of your savings.

3. Add or subtract the numbers for the respective month as necessary.

4. At the end of the month transfer the new Savings Account Balance to top of the Savings Balance column of the next month.

savings plan + TRACKER

	JAN	FEB	MAR	APR	MAY	JUN	JULY	AUG	SEPT	OCT	NOV	DEC
CURRENT SAVINGS BALANCE												
MONTHLY SAVINGS												
MONEY ADDED/WITHDRAWN												
SAVINGS ACCOUNT BALANCE												

savings plan + TRACKER

	JAN	FEB	MAR	APR	MAY	JUN	JULY	AUG	SEPT	OCT	NOV	DEC
CURRENT SAVINGS BALANCE												
MONTHLY SAVINGS												
MONEY ADDED/WITHDRAWN												
SAVINGS ACCOUNT BALANCE												

FAMILY
finances

FAMILY *financial* INVENTORY

Name:
Relationship:
Date of Birth:
Have a Will? (Yes or No)

RELATIVE HAS BANK ACCOUNTS WITH:

NAME OF BANK	ACCOUNT #	ACCOUNT TYPE

RELATIVE HAS INVESTMENT ACCOUNTS WITH:

INVESTMENT COMPANY	ACCOUNT #	ACCOUNT TYPE

RELATIVE HAS RETIREMENT ACCOUNTS WITH:

RETIREMENT ACCOUNT NAME	ACCOUNT #	ACCOUNT TYPE

FAMILY *financial* INVENTORY

RELATIVE HAS LIFE INSURANCE WITH:

NAME OF BANK	ACCOUNT #	ACCOUNT TYPE

RELATIVE HAS OTHER INSURANCES WITH:

INVESTMENT COMPANY	ACCOUNT #	ACCOUNT TYPE

RELATIVE HAS PERSONAL PROPERTY:

PROPERTY DESCRIPTION	VALUE	OTHER INFO

FAMILY *financial* INVENTORY

Name:
Relationship:
Date of Birth:
Have a Will? (Yes or No)

RELATIVE HAS BANK ACCOUNTS WITH:

NAME OF BANK	ACCOUNT #	ACCOUNT TYPE

RELATIVE HAS INVESTMENT ACCOUNTS WITH:

INVESTMENT COMPANY	ACCOUNT #	ACCOUNT TYPE

RELATIVE HAS RETIREMENT ACCOUNTS WITH:

RETIREMENT ACCOUNT NAME	ACCOUNT #	ACCOUNT TYPE

FAMILY *financial* INVENTORY

RELATIVE HAS LIFE INSURANCE WITH:

NAME OF BANK	ACCOUNT #	ACCOUNT TYPE

RELATIVE HAS OTHER INSURANCES WITH:

INVESTMENT COMPANY	ACCOUNT #	ACCOUNT TYPE

RELATIVE HAS PERSONAL PROPERTY:

PROPERTY DESCRIPTION	VALUE	OTHER INFO

FAMILY *financial* INVENTORY

Name:
Relationship:
Date of Birth:
Have a Will? (Yes or No)

RELATIVE HAS BANK ACCOUNTS WITH:

NAME OF BANK	ACCOUNT #	ACCOUNT TYPE

RELATIVE HAS INVESTMENT ACCOUNTS WITH:

INVESTMENT COMPANY	ACCOUNT #	ACCOUNT TYPE

RELATIVE HAS RETIREMENT ACCOUNTS WITH:

RETIREMENT ACCOUNT NAME	ACCOUNT #	ACCOUNT TYPE

FAMILY *financial* INVENTORY

RELATIVE HAS LIFE INSURANCE WITH:

NAME OF BANK	ACCOUNT #	ACCOUNT TYPE

RELATIVE HAS OTHER INSURANCES WITH:

INVESTMENT COMPANY	ACCOUNT #	ACCOUNT TYPE

RELATIVE HAS PERSONAL PROPERTY:

PROPERTY DESCRIPTION	VALUE	OTHER INFO

FAMILY
financial
INVENTORY

Name:
Relationship:
Date of Birth:
Have a Will? (Yes or No)

RELATIVE HAS BANK ACCOUNTS WITH:

NAME OF BANK	ACCOUNT #	ACCOUNT TYPE

RELATIVE HAS INVESTMENT ACCOUNTS WITH:

INVESTMENT COMPANY	ACCOUNT #	ACCOUNT TYPE

RELATIVE HAS RETIREMENT ACCOUNTS WITH:

RETIREMENT ACCOUNT NAME	ACCOUNT #	ACCOUNT TYPE

FAMILY *financial* INVENTORY

RELATIVE HAS LIFE INSURANCE WITH:

NAME OF BANK	ACCOUNT #	ACCOUNT TYPE

RELATIVE HAS OTHER INSURANCES WITH:

INVESTMENT COMPANY	ACCOUNT #	ACCOUNT TYPE

RELATIVE HAS PERSONAL PROPERTY:

PROPERTY DESCRIPTION	VALUE	OTHER INFO

FAMILY *financial* INVENTORY

Name:
Relationship:
Date of Birth:
Have a Will? (Yes or No)

RELATIVE HAS BANK ACCOUNTS WITH:

NAME OF BANK	ACCOUNT #	ACCOUNT TYPE

RELATIVE HAS INVESTMENT ACCOUNTS WITH:

INVESTMENT COMPANY	ACCOUNT #	ACCOUNT TYPE

RELATIVE HAS RETIREMENT ACCOUNTS WITH:

RETIREMENT ACCOUNT NAME	ACCOUNT #	ACCOUNT TYPE

FAMILY *financial* INVENTORY

RELATIVE HAS LIFE INSURANCE WITH:

NAME OF BANK	ACCOUNT #	ACCOUNT TYPE

RELATIVE HAS OTHER INSURANCES WITH:

INVESTMENT COMPANY	ACCOUNT #	ACCOUNT TYPE

RELATIVE HAS PERSONAL PROPERTY:

PROPERTY DESCRIPTION	VALUE	OTHER INFO